AF481697

ABOUT THE MILKY WAY (OUR HOME GALAXY): 3RD GRADE SCIENCE TEXTBOOK SERIES

Speedy Publishing LLC
40 E. Main St. #1156
Newark, DE 19711
www.speedypublishing.com

Copyright 2015

All Rights reserved. No part of this book may be reproduced or used in any way or form or by any means whether electronic or mechanical, this means that you cannot record or photocopy any material ideas or tips that are provided in this book

The Milky Way is one of many galaxies that lie in the universe. The Milky Way Galaxy is our home galaxy in the universe.

The Milky Way began forming around 12 billion years ago. The Milky Way is part of cluster of around 3,000 galaxies called the Local Group.

The Milky Way
is made up of at
least 100 billion
stars, as well as
dust and gas. The
center of the Milky
Way contains a
black hole that
sucks up anything
that crosses it.

The Milky Way
is so named
because across
the night sky,
it has a milky
appearance.

The Milky Way
is very big and
takes about 200
million years
to make one
complete rotation.

The closest galaxy
to the Milky Way
is Andromeda,
which is around
2.6 million light
years away
from us.

It takes over two
hundred million
years for the sun
to orbit the center
of the galaxy.
This is called a
galactic year.

More than half
the stars found
in the Milky Way
are older than
the 4.5 billion
year old sun.

www.ingramcontent.com/pod-product-compliance
Lightning Source LLC
Chambersburg PA
CBHW060621120726
48002CB00010B/3056